LIBRARY LENDING JOURNAL

FOR BOOKS, DVDs, TOOLS, ETC..

WITH THOUGHTFUL QUOTATIONS

this book belongs to

address

____

____

____

____

phone

office ______________________

cell ________________________

____

Designed by Clara Brayton

JANUARY 2025
ISBN 9781966630043

"Through the magic of six dots the gates of knowledge have been flung wide, and the blind of each country can enter the world of enchantment beyond the reach of physical sense. Never at any time are we so free as when we hold a beloved book on our knee, and the Braille dots flash into our fingers the greatness, the wonder, the boundlessness of life."

Helen Keller (1930)

RULES FOR BORROWING MY BOOKS

- ***No dog ears on pages***
- ***No eating food over book***
- ***No drinking over book***
- ***No writing or highlighting***
- ***No ripping pages***
- ***Do not lend to others***
- ***Return in same condition as borrowed.***

BORROWER AND INFO	ITEM LOANED

NOTES	CONDITION OF ITEM
DATE OUT DATE BACK	P G F E OUT ☐☐☐☐ BACK ☐☐☐☐ LOAN TO AGAIN Y ☐ N ☐

BORROWER AND INFO	ITEM LOANED

NOTES	CONDITION OF ITEM
DATE OUT DATE BACK	P G F E OUT ☐☐☐☐ BACK ☐☐☐☐ LOAN TO AGAIN Y ☐ N ☐

"There is no friend as loyal as a book."
Ernest Hemingway

KEY FOR CONDITION OF ITEM P=POOR G=GOOD F=FAIR E=EXCELLENT

BORROWER AND INFO	ITEM LOANED

NOTES	CONDITION OF ITEM
DATE OUT DATE BACK	P G F E OUT ☐ ☐ ☐ ☐ BACK ☐ ☐ ☐ ☐ LOAN TO AGAIN Y ☐ N ☐

BORROWER AND INFO	ITEM LOANED

NOTES	CONDITION OF ITEM
DATE OUT DATE BACK	P G F E OUT ☐ ☐ ☐ ☐ BACK ☐ ☐ ☐ ☐ LOAN TO AGAIN Y ☐ N ☐

KEY FOR CONDITION OF ITEM P=POOR G=GOOD F=FAIR E=EXCELLENT

BORROWER AND INFO	ITEM LOANED

NOTES	CONDITION OF ITEM
DATE OUT DATE BACK	P G F E OUT ☐☐☐☐ BACK ☐☐☐☐ LOAN TO AGAIN Y ☐ N ☐

BORROWER AND INFO	ITEM LOANED

NOTES	CONDITION OF ITEM
DATE OUT DATE BACK	P G F E OUT ☐☐☐☐ BACK ☐☐☐☐ LOAN TO AGAIN Y ☐ N ☐

"Lending books to other people is merely a shrewd form of housecleaning." Joe Queenan

KEY FOR CONDITION OF ITEM P=POOR G=GOOD F=FAIR E=EXCELLENT

BORROWER AND INFO

ITEM LOANED

NOTES

DATE OUT

DATE BACK

CONDITION OF ITEM

	P	G	F	E
OUT				
BACK				

LOAN TO AGAIN Y N

BORROWER AND INFO

ITEM LOANED

NOTES

DATE OUT

DATE BACK

CONDITION OF ITEM

	P	G	F	E
OUT				
BACK				

LOAN TO AGAIN Y N

KEY FOR CONDITION OF ITEM P=POOR G=GOOD F=FAIR E=EXCELLENT

BORROWER AND INFO	ITEM LOANED

NOTES	CONDITION OF ITEM
DATE OUT DATE BACK	P G F E OUT BACK LOAN TO AGAIN Y N

BORROWER AND INFO	ITEM LOANED

NOTES	CONDITION OF ITEM
DATE OUT DATE BACK	P G F E OUT BACK LOAN TO AGAIN Y N

"People are much more willing to lend books than bookcases." Mark Twain

KEY FOR CONDITION OF ITEM P=POOR G=GOOD F=FAIR E=EXCELLENT

BORROWER AND INFO	ITEM LOANED

NOTES	CONDITION OF ITEM
DATE OUT DATE BACK	P G F E OUT ☐ ☐ ☐ ☐ BACK ☐ ☐ ☐ ☐ LOAN TO AGAIN Y ☐ N ☐

BORROWER AND INFO	ITEM LOANED

NOTES	CONDITION OF ITEM
DATE OUT DATE BACK	P G F E OUT ☐ ☐ ☐ ☐ BACK ☐ ☐ ☐ ☐ LOAN TO AGAIN Y ☐ N ☐

KEY FOR CONDITION OF ITEM P=POOR G=GOOD F=FAIR E=EXCELLENT

BORROWER AND INFO

ITEM LOANED

NOTES

DATE OUT

DATE BACK

CONDITION OF ITEM

	P	G	F	E
OUT				
BACK				
LOAN TO AGAIN	Y		N	

BORROWER AND INFO

ITEM LOANED

NOTES

DATE OUT

DATE BACK

CONDITION OF ITEM

	P	G	F	E
OUT				
BACK				
LOAN TO AGAIN	Y		N	

"Some books are to be tasted, others to be swallowed, and some few to be chewed and digested." Sir Francis Bacon

KEY FOR CONDITION OF ITEM P=POOR G=GOOD F=FAIR E=EXCELLENT

BORROWER AND INFO | ITEM LOANED

NOTES

DATE OUT

DATE BACK

CONDITION OF ITEM

	P	G	F	E
OUT				
BACK				

LOAN TO AGAIN Y N

BORROWER AND INFO | ITEM LOANED

NOTES

DATE OUT

DATE BACK

CONDITION OF ITEM

	P	G	F	E
OUT				
BACK				

LOAN TO AGAIN Y N

KEY FOR CONDITION OF ITEM P=POOR G=GOOD F=FAIR E=EXCELLENT

BORROWER AND INFO | ITEM LOANED

NOTES

DATE OUT

DATE BACK

CONDITION OF ITEM

	P	G	F	E
OUT				
BACK				

LOAN TO AGAIN Y N

BORROWER AND INFO | ITEM LOANED

NOTES

DATE OUT

DATE BACK

CONDITION OF ITEM

	P	G	F	E
OUT				
BACK				

LOAN TO AGAIN Y N

"Neither a borrower nor a lender be."
Benjamin Franklin or Hamlet Act One, Scene Three

KEY FOR CONDITION OF ITEM P=POOR G=GOOD F=FAIR E=EXCELLENT

BORROWER AND INFO	ITEM LOANED

NOTES	CONDITION OF ITEM
DATE OUT DATE BACK	P G F E OUT BACK LOAN TO AGAIN Y N

BORROWER AND INFO	ITEM LOANED

NOTES	CONDITION OF ITEM
DATE OUT DATE BACK	P G F E OUT BACK LOAN TO AGAIN Y N

KEY FOR CONDITION OF ITEM P=POOR G=GOOD F=FAIR E=EXCELLENT

BORROWER AND INFO	ITEM LOANED

NOTES	CONDITION OF ITEM
DATE OUT DATE BACK	P G F E OUT BACK LOAN TO AGAIN Y N

BORROWER AND INFO	ITEM LOANED

NOTES	CONDITION OF ITEM
DATE OUT DATE BACK	P G F E OUT BACK LOAN TO AGAIN Y N

"A room without books is like a body without a soul."
Marcus Tillius Cicero

KEY FOR CONDITION OF ITEM P=POOR G=GOOD F=FAIR E=EXCELLENT

BORROWER AND INFO	ITEM LOANED

NOTES	CONDITION OF ITEM
DATE OUT DATE BACK	P G F E OUT ☐ ☐ ☐ ☐ BACK ☐ ☐ ☐ ☐ LOAN TO AGAIN Y ☐ N ☐

BORROWER AND INFO	ITEM LOANED

NOTES	CONDITION OF ITEM
DATE OUT DATE BACK	P G F E OUT ☐ ☐ ☐ ☐ BACK ☐ ☐ ☐ ☐ LOAN TO AGAIN Y ☐ N ☐

KEY FOR CONDITION OF ITEM P=POOR G=GOOD F=FAIR E=EXCELLENT

BORROWER AND INFO	ITEM LOANED

NOTES	CONDITION OF ITEM
DATE OUT DATE BACK	P G F E OUT ☐ ☐ ☐ ☐ BACK ☐ ☐ ☐ ☐ LOAN TO AGAIN Y ☐ N ☐

BORROWER AND INFO	ITEM LOANED

NOTES	CONDITION OF ITEM
DATE OUT DATE BACK	P G F E OUT ☐ ☐ ☐ ☐ BACK ☐ ☐ ☐ ☐ LOAN TO AGAIN Y ☐ N ☐

"Books are uniquely portable magic." Stephen King

KEY FOR CONDITION OF ITEM P=POOR G=GOOD F=FAIR E=EXCELLENT

BORROWER AND INFO	ITEM LOANED

NOTES	CONDITION OF ITEM
DATE OUT DATE BACK	P G F E OUT ☐☐☐☐ BACK ☐☐☐☐ LOAN TO AGAIN Y ☐ N ☐

BORROWER AND INFO	ITEM LOANED

NOTES	CONDITION OF ITEM
DATE OUT DATE BACK	P G F E OUT ☐☐☐☐ BACK ☐☐☐☐ LOAN TO AGAIN Y ☐ N ☐

KEY FOR CONDITION OF ITEM P=POOR G=GOOD F=FAIR E=EXCELLENT

BORROWER AND INFO	ITEM LOANED

NOTES	CONDITION OF ITEM
DATE OUT DATE BACK	P G F E OUT BACK LOAN TO AGAIN Y N

BORROWER AND INFO	ITEM LOANED

NOTES	CONDITION OF ITEM
DATE OUT DATE BACK	P G F E OUT BACK LOAN TO AGAIN Y N

"I think books are like people, in the sense that they'll turn up in your life when you need them." Emma Thompson

KEY FOR CONDITION OF ITEM P=POOR G=GOOD F=FAIR E=EXCELLENT

BORROWER AND INFO	ITEM LOANED

NOTES	CONDITION OF ITEM
DATE OUT DATE BACK	P G F E OUT ☐☐☐☐ BACK ☐☐☐☐ LOAN TO AGAIN Y ☐ N ☐

BORROWER AND INFO	ITEM LOANED

NOTES	CONDITION OF ITEM
DATE OUT DATE BACK	P G F E OUT ☐☐☐☐ BACK ☐☐☐☐ LOAN TO AGAIN Y ☐ N ☐

KEY FOR CONDITION OF ITEM P=POOR G=GOOD F=FAIR E=EXCELLENT

BORROWER AND INFO	ITEM LOANED

NOTES	CONDITION OF ITEM
DATE OUT DATE BACK	P G F E OUT ☐ ☐ ☐ ☐ BACK ☐ ☐ ☐ ☐ LOAN TO AGAIN Y ☐ N ☐

BORROWER AND INFO	ITEM LOANED

NOTES	CONDITION OF ITEM
DATE OUT DATE BACK	P G F E OUT ☐ ☐ ☐ ☐ BACK ☐ ☐ ☐ ☐ LOAN TO AGAIN Y ☐ N ☐

"Today a reader, tomorrow a leader."

Margaret Atwood

KEY FOR CONDITION OF ITEM P=POOR G=GOOD F=FAIR E=EXCELLENT

BORROWER AND INFO

ITEM LOANED

NOTES

DATE OUT

DATE BACK

CONDITION OF ITEM

	P	G	F	E
OUT				
BACK				
LOAN TO AGAIN	Y		N	

BORROWER AND INFO

ITEM LOANED

NOTES

DATE OUT

DATE BACK

CONDITION OF ITEM

	P	G	F	E
OUT				
BACK				
LOAN TO AGAIN	Y		N	

KEY FOR CONDITION OF ITEM P=POOR G=GOOD F=FAIR E=EXCELLENT

BORROWER AND INFO	ITEM LOANED

NOTES	CONDITION OF ITEM				
DATE OUT DATE BACK		P	G	F	E
	OUT				
	BACK				
	LOAN TO AGAIN	Y		N	

BORROWER AND INFO	ITEM LOANED

NOTES	CONDITION OF ITEM				
DATE OUT DATE BACK		P	G	F	E
	OUT				
	BACK				
	LOAN TO AGAIN	Y		N	

"If you don't like to read, you haven't found the right book." J.K. Rowling

KEY FOR CONDITION OF ITEM P=POOR G=GOOD F=FAIR E=EXCELLENT

BORROWER AND INFO	ITEM LOANED

NOTES	CONDITION OF ITEM
DATE OUT DATE BACK	P G F E OUT BACK LOAN TO AGAIN Y N

BORROWER AND INFO	ITEM LOANED

NOTES	CONDITION OF ITEM
DATE OUT DATE BACK	P G F E OUT BACK LOAN TO AGAIN Y N

KEY FOR CONDITION OF ITEM P=POOR G=GOOD F=FAIR E=EXCELLENT

BORROWER AND INFO

ITEM LOANED

NOTES

DATE OUT

DATE BACK

CONDITION OF ITEM

	P	G	F	E
OUT				
BACK				

LOAN TO AGAIN Y N

BORROWER AND INFO

ITEM LOANED

NOTES

DATE OUT

DATE BACK

CONDITION OF ITEM

	P	G	F	E
OUT				
BACK				

LOAN TO AGAIN Y N

"I guess there are never enough books."
John Steinbeck

KEY FOR CONDITION OF ITEM P=POOR G=GOOD F=FAIR E=EXCELLENT

BORROWER AND INFO	ITEM LOANED

NOTES	CONDITION OF ITEM
DATE OUT DATE BACK	P G F E OUT ☐☐☐☐ BACK ☐☐☐☐ LOAN TO AGAIN Y ☐ N ☐

BORROWER AND INFO	ITEM LOANED

NOTES	CONDITION OF ITEM
DATE OUT DATE BACK	P G F E OUT ☐☐☐☐ BACK ☐☐☐☐ LOAN TO AGAIN Y ☐ N ☐

KEY FOR CONDITION OF ITEM P=POOR G=GOOD F=FAIR E=EXCELLENT

BORROWER AND INFO	ITEM LOANED

NOTES	CONDITION OF ITEM
DATE OUT DATE BACK	P G F E OUT BACK LOAN TO AGAIN Y N

BORROWER AND INFO	ITEM LOANED

NOTES	CONDITION OF ITEM
DATE OUT DATE BACK	P G F E OUT BACK LOAN TO AGAIN Y N

***"Despite the enormous quantity of books, how few people read! And if one reads profitably, one would realize how much stupid stuff the vulgar herd is content to swallow every day."* Voltaire**

KEY FOR CONDITION OF ITEM P=POOR G=GOOD F=FAIR E=EXCELLENT

BORROWER AND INFO	ITEM LOANED

NOTES	CONDITION OF ITEM
DATE OUT DATE BACK	

	P	G	F	E
OUT				
BACK				

LOAN TO AGAIN	Y		N	

BORROWER AND INFO	ITEM LOANED

NOTES	CONDITION OF ITEM
DATE OUT DATE BACK	

	P	G	F	E
OUT				
BACK				

LOAN TO AGAIN	Y		N	

KEY FOR CONDITION OF ITEM P=POOR G=GOOD F=FAIR E=EXCELLENT

BORROWER AND INFO	ITEM LOANED

NOTES	CONDITION OF ITEM
DATE OUT DATE BACK	P G F E OUT ☐☐☐☐ BACK ☐☐☐☐ LOAN TO AGAIN Y ☐ N ☐

BORROWER AND INFO	ITEM LOANED

NOTES	CONDITION OF ITEM
DATE OUT DATE BACK	P G F E OUT ☐☐☐☐ BACK ☐☐☐☐ LOAN TO AGAIN Y ☐ N ☐

"The world is a stage, but the play is badly cast."
Oscar Wilde

KEY FOR CONDITION OF ITEM P=POOR G=GOOD F=FAIR E=EXCELLENT

BORROWER AND INFO	ITEM LOANED

NOTES	CONDITION OF ITEM
DATE OUT DATE BACK	P G F E OUT BACK LOAN TO AGAIN Y N

BORROWER AND INFO	ITEM LOANED

NOTES	CONDITION OF ITEM
DATE OUT DATE BACK	P G F E OUT BACK LOAN TO AGAIN Y N

KEY FOR CONDITION OF ITEM P=POOR G=GOOD F=FAIR E=EXCELLENT

BORROWER AND INFO	ITEM LOANED

NOTES	CONDITION OF ITEM
DATE OUT DATE BACK	P G F E OUT BACK LOAN TO AGAIN Y N

BORROWER AND INFO	ITEM LOANED

NOTES	CONDITION OF ITEM
DATE OUT DATE BACK	P G F E OUT BACK LOAN TO AGAIN Y N

"Happiness is starting a new book." unknown & many

KEY FOR CONDITION OF ITEM P=POOR G=GOOD F=FAIR E=EXCELLENT

BORROWER AND INFO	ITEM LOANED

NOTES	CONDITION OF ITEM
DATE OUT DATE BACK	P G F E OUT ☐ ☐ ☐ ☐ BACK ☐ ☐ ☐ ☐ LOAN TO AGAIN Y ☐ N ☐

BORROWER AND INFO	ITEM LOANED

NOTES	CONDITION OF ITEM
DATE OUT DATE BACK	P G F E OUT ☐ ☐ ☐ ☐ BACK ☐ ☐ ☐ ☐ LOAN TO AGAIN Y ☐ N ☐

KEY FOR CONDITION OF ITEM P=POOR G=GOOD F=FAIR E=EXCELLENT

BORROWER AND INFO	ITEM LOANED

NOTES	CONDITION OF ITEM
DATE OUT DATE BACK	P G F E OUT BACK LOAN TO AGAIN Y N

BORROWER AND INFO	ITEM LOANED

NOTES	CONDITION OF ITEM
DATE OUT DATE BACK	P G F E OUT BACK LOAN TO AGAIN Y N

"She reads books as one who breathes air, to fill up and live." Annie Dillard

KEY FOR CONDITION OF ITEM P=POOR G=GOOD F=FAIR E=EXCELLENT

BORROWER AND INFO	ITEM LOANED

NOTES	CONDITION OF ITEM
DATE OUT DATE BACK	P G F E OUT ☐☐☐☐ BACK ☐☐☐☐ LOAN TO AGAIN Y ☐ N ☐

BORROWER AND INFO	ITEM LOANED

NOTES	CONDITION OF ITEM
DATE OUT DATE BACK	P G F E OUT ☐☐☐☐ BACK ☐☐☐☐ LOAN TO AGAIN Y ☐ N ☐

KEY FOR CONDITION OF ITEM P=POOR G=GOOD F=FAIR E=EXCELLENT

BORROWER AND INFO	ITEM LOANED

NOTES	CONDITION OF ITEM
DATE OUT DATE BACK	P G F E OUT ☐ ☐ ☐ ☐ BACK ☐ ☐ ☐ ☐ LOAN TO AGAIN Y ☐ N ☐

BORROWER AND INFO	ITEM LOANED

NOTES	CONDITION OF ITEM
DATE OUT DATE BACK	P G F E OUT ☐ ☐ ☐ ☐ BACK ☐ ☐ ☐ ☐ LOAN TO AGAIN Y ☐ N ☐

"Why yes I'm addicted to reading, but at least I'm minding my own business." Jamie E. Davis

KEY FOR CONDITION OF ITEM P=POOR G=GOOD F=FAIR E=EXCELLENT

BORROWER AND INFO	ITEM LOANED

NOTES	CONDITION OF ITEM
DATE OUT DATE BACK	P G F E OUT ☐☐☐☐ BACK ☐☐☐☐ LOAN TO AGAIN Y ☐ N ☐

BORROWER AND INFO	ITEM LOANED

NOTES	CONDITION OF ITEM
DATE OUT DATE BACK	P G F E OUT ☐☐☐☐ BACK ☐☐☐☐ LOAN TO AGAIN Y ☐ N ☐

KEY FOR CONDITION OF ITEM P=POOR G=GOOD F=FAIR E=EXCELLENT

BORROWER AND INFO	ITEM LOANED

NOTES	CONDITION OF ITEM
DATE OUT DATE BACK	P G F E OUT ☐☐☐☐ BACK ☐☐☐☐ LOAN TO AGAIN Y ☐ N ☐

BORROWER AND INFO	ITEM LOANED

NOTES	CONDITION OF ITEM
DATE OUT DATE BACK	P G F E OUT ☐☐☐☐ BACK ☐☐☐☐ LOAN TO AGAIN Y ☐ N ☐

***"Keep reading. It's one of the most marvelous adventures anyone can have."* Lloyd Alexander**

KEY FOR CONDITION OF ITEM P=POOR G=GOOD F=FAIR E=EXCELLENT

BORROWER AND INFO	ITEM LOANED

NOTES	CONDITION OF ITEM
DATE OUT DATE BACK	P G F E OUT BACK LOAN TO AGAIN Y N

BORROWER AND INFO	ITEM LOANED

NOTES	CONDITION OF ITEM
DATE OUT DATE BACK	P G F E OUT BACK LOAN TO AGAIN Y N

KEY FOR CONDITION OF ITEM P=POOR G=GOOD F=FAIR E=EXCELLENT

BORROWER AND INFO | ITEM LOANED

NOTES

DATE OUT

DATE BACK

CONDITION OF ITEM

	P	G	F	E
OUT				
BACK				
LOAN TO AGAIN	Y		N	

BORROWER AND INFO | ITEM LOANED

NOTES

DATE OUT

DATE BACK

CONDITION OF ITEM

	P	G	F	E
OUT				
BACK				
LOAN TO AGAIN	Y		N	

"The only thing you absolutely have to know is the location of the library." Albert Einstein

KEY FOR CONDITION OF ITEM P=POOR G=GOOD F=FAIR E=EXCELLENT

BORROWER AND INFO	ITEM LOANED

NOTES	CONDITION OF ITEM
DATE OUT DATE BACK	P G F E OUT ☐☐☐☐ BACK ☐☐☐☐ LOAN TO AGAIN Y ☐ N ☐

BORROWER AND INFO	ITEM LOANED

NOTES	CONDITION OF ITEM
DATE OUT DATE BACK	P G F E OUT ☐☐☐☐ BACK ☐☐☐☐ LOAN TO AGAIN Y ☐ N ☐

KEY FOR CONDITION OF ITEM P=POOR G=GOOD F=FAIR E=EXCELLENT

BORROWER AND INFO

ITEM LOANED

NOTES

DATE OUT

DATE BACK

CONDITION OF ITEM

	P	G	F	E
OUT				
BACK				

LOAN TO AGAIN Y N

BORROWER AND INFO

ITEM LOANED

NOTES

DATE OUT

DATE BACK

CONDITION OF ITEM

	P	G	F	E
OUT				
BACK				

LOAN TO AGAIN Y N

"More than at any other time, when I hold a beloved book in my hand my limitations fall from me, my spirit is free."
Helen Keller

KEY FOR CONDITION OF ITEM P=POOR G=GOOD F=FAIR E=EXCELLENT

BORROWER AND INFO	ITEM LOANED

NOTES	CONDITION OF ITEM
DATE OUT DATE BACK	

	P	G	F	E
OUT				
BACK				
LOAN TO AGAIN	Y		N	

BORROWER AND INFO	ITEM LOANED

NOTES	CONDITION OF ITEM
DATE OUT DATE BACK	

	P	G	F	E
OUT				
BACK				
LOAN TO AGAIN	Y		N	

KEY FOR CONDITION OF ITEM P=POOR G=GOOD F=FAIR E=EXCELLENT

BORROWER AND INFO	ITEM LOANED

NOTES	CONDITION OF ITEM				
DATE OUT DATE BACK		P	G	F	E
	OUT				
	BACK				
	LOAN TO AGAIN	Y		N	

BORROWER AND INFO	ITEM LOANED

NOTES	CONDITION OF ITEM				
DATE OUT DATE BACK		P	G	F	E
	OUT				
	BACK				
	LOAN TO AGAIN	Y		N	

"Reading should not be presented to children as a chore, a duty. It should be offered as a gift." Kate DiCamillo

KEY FOR CONDITION OF ITEM P=POOR G=GOOD F=FAIR E=EXCELLENT

BORROWER AND INFO	ITEM LOANED

NOTES	CONDITION OF ITEM
DATE OUT DATE BACK	P G F E OUT ☐ ☐ ☐ ☐ BACK ☐ ☐ ☐ ☐ LOAN TO AGAIN Y ☐ N ☐

BORROWER AND INFO	ITEM LOANED

NOTES	CONDITION OF ITEM
DATE OUT DATE BACK	P G F E OUT ☐ ☐ ☐ ☐ BACK ☐ ☐ ☐ ☐ LOAN TO AGAIN Y ☐ N ☐

KEY FOR CONDITION OF ITEM P=POOR G=GOOD F=FAIR E=EXCELLENT

BORROWER AND INFO	ITEM LOANED

NOTES	CONDITION OF ITEM				
DATE OUT		P	G	F	E
DATE BACK	OUT				
	BACK				
	LOAN TO AGAIN	Y		N	

BORROWER AND INFO	ITEM LOANED

NOTES	CONDITION OF ITEM				
DATE OUT		P	G	F	E
DATE BACK	OUT				
	BACK				
	LOAN TO AGAIN	Y		N	

"Reading gives us someplace to go when we have to stay where we are." Mason Cooley

KEY FOR CONDITION OF ITEM P=POOR G=GOOD F=FAIR E=EXCELLENT

BORROWER AND INFO	ITEM LOANED

NOTES	CONDITION OF ITEM
DATE OUT DATE BACK	P G F E OUT ☐ ☐ ☐ ☐ BACK ☐ ☐ ☐ ☐ LOAN TO AGAIN Y ☐ N ☐

BORROWER AND INFO	ITEM LOANED

NOTES	CONDITION OF ITEM
DATE OUT DATE BACK	P G F E OUT ☐ ☐ ☐ ☐ BACK ☐ ☐ ☐ ☐ LOAN TO AGAIN Y ☐ N ☐

KEY FOR CONDITION OF ITEM P=POOR G=GOOD F=FAIR E=EXCELLENT

BORROWER AND INFO	ITEM LOANED

NOTES	CONDITION OF ITEM	P	G	F	E
DATE OUT	OUT				
DATE BACK	BACK				
	LOAN TO AGAIN	Y		N	

BORROWER AND INFO	ITEM LOANED

NOTES	CONDITION OF ITEM	P	G	F	E
DATE OUT	OUT				
DATE BACK	BACK				
	LOAN TO AGAIN	Y		N	

“There is no Frigate like a Book To take us Lands away.”
Emily Dickinson

KEY FOR CONDITION OF ITEM P=POOR G=GOOD F=FAIR E=EXCELLENT

BORROWER AND INFO	ITEM LOANED

NOTES	CONDITION OF ITEM
DATE OUT DATE BACK	

	P	G	F	E
OUT				
BACK				
LOAN TO AGAIN	Y		N	

BORROWER AND INFO	ITEM LOANED

NOTES	CONDITION OF ITEM
DATE OUT DATE BACK	

	P	G	F	E
OUT				
BACK				
LOAN TO AGAIN	Y		N	

KEY FOR CONDITION OF ITEM P=POOR G=GOOD F=FAIR E=EXCELLENT

BORROWER AND INFO	ITEM LOANED

NOTES	CONDITION OF ITEM
DATE OUT DATE BACK	P G F E OUT ☐ ☐ ☐ ☐ BACK ☐ ☐ ☐ ☐ LOAN TO AGAIN Y ☐ N ☐

BORROWER AND INFO	ITEM LOANED

NOTES	CONDITION OF ITEM
DATE OUT DATE BACK	P G F E OUT ☐ ☐ ☐ ☐ BACK ☐ ☐ ☐ ☐ LOAN TO AGAIN Y ☐ N ☐

"Books are mirrors: You only see in them what you already have inside you." Carlos Ruiz Zafón

KEY FOR CONDITION OF ITEM P=POOR G=GOOD F=FAIR E=EXCELLENT

BORROWER AND INFO	ITEM LOANED

NOTES	CONDITION OF ITEM				
DATE OUT DATE BACK		P	G	F	E
	OUT				
	BACK				
	LOAN TO AGAIN	Y		N	

BORROWER AND INFO	ITEM LOANED

NOTES	CONDITION OF ITEM				
DATE OUT DATE BACK		P	G	F	E
	OUT				
	BACK				
	LOAN TO AGAIN	Y		N	

KEY FOR CONDITION OF ITEM P=POOR G=GOOD F=FAIR E=EXCELLENT

BORROWER AND INFO	ITEM LOANED

NOTES	CONDITION OF ITEM
DATE OUT DATE BACK	P G F E OUT ☐☐☐☐ BACK ☐☐☐☐ LOAN TO AGAIN Y ☐ N ☐

BORROWER AND INFO	ITEM LOANED

NOTES	CONDITION OF ITEM
DATE OUT DATE BACK	P G F E OUT ☐☐☐☐ BACK ☐☐☐☐ LOAN TO AGAIN Y ☐ N ☐

***"A reader lives a thousand lives before he dies . . . The man who never reads lives only one."* George R.R. Martin**

KEY FOR CONDITION OF ITEM P=POOR G=GOOD F=FAIR E=EXCELLENT

BORROWER AND INFO	ITEM LOANED

NOTES	CONDITION OF ITEM
DATE OUT DATE BACK	P G F E OUT ☐☐☐☐ BACK ☐☐☐☐ LOAN TO AGAIN Y ☐ N ☐

BORROWER AND INFO	ITEM LOANED

NOTES	CONDITION OF ITEM
DATE OUT DATE BACK	P G F E OUT ☐☐☐☐ BACK ☐☐☐☐ LOAN TO AGAIN Y ☐ N ☐

KEY FOR CONDITION OF ITEM P=POOR G=GOOD F=FAIR E=EXCELLENT

BORROWER AND INFO	ITEM LOANED

NOTES	CONDITION OF ITEM
DATE OUT DATE BACK	P G F E OUT ☐ ☐ ☐ ☐ BACK ☐ ☐ ☐ ☐ LOAN TO AGAIN Y ☐ N ☐

BORROWER AND INFO	ITEM LOANED

NOTES	CONDITION OF ITEM
DATE OUT DATE BACK	P G F E OUT ☐ ☐ ☐ ☐ BACK ☐ ☐ ☐ ☐ LOAN TO AGAIN Y ☐ N ☐

"A book, too, can be a star, a living fire to lighten the darkness, leading out into the expanding universe."
Madeleine L'Engle

KEY FOR CONDITION OF ITEM P=POOR G=GOOD F=FAIR E=EXCELLENT

BORROWER AND INFO	ITEM LOANED

NOTES	CONDITION OF ITEM
DATE OUT DATE BACK	P G F E OUT BACK LOAN TO AGAIN Y N

BORROWER AND INFO	ITEM LOANED

NOTES	CONDITION OF ITEM
DATE OUT DATE BACK	P G F E OUT BACK LOAN TO AGAIN Y N

KEY FOR CONDITION OF ITEM P=POOR G=GOOD F=FAIR E=EXCELLENT

BORROWER AND INFO	ITEM LOANED

NOTES	CONDITION OF ITEM
DATE OUT DATE BACK	P G F E OUT ☐ ☐ ☐ ☐ BACK ☐ ☐ ☐ ☐ LOAN TO AGAIN Y ☐ N ☐

BORROWER AND INFO	ITEM LOANED

NOTES	CONDITION OF ITEM
DATE OUT DATE BACK	P G F E OUT ☐ ☐ ☐ ☐ BACK ☐ ☐ ☐ ☐ LOAN TO AGAIN Y ☐ N ☐

"A book is a dream that you hold in your hand."
Neil Gaiman

KEY FOR CONDITION OF ITEM P=POOR G=GOOD F=FAIR E=EXCELLENT

BORROWER AND INFO	ITEM LOANED

NOTES	CONDITION OF ITEM				
DATE OUT DATE BACK		P	G	F	E
	OUT				
	BACK				
	LOAN TO AGAIN	Y		N	

BORROWER AND INFO	ITEM LOANED

NOTES	CONDITION OF ITEM				
DATE OUT DATE BACK		P	G	F	E
	OUT				
	BACK				
	LOAN TO AGAIN	Y		N	

KEY FOR CONDITION OF ITEM P=POOR G=GOOD F=FAIR E=EXCELLENT

BORROWER AND INFO | ITEM LOANED

NOTES | CONDITION OF ITEM

DATE OUT

DATE BACK

		P	G	F	E
OUT					
BACK					
LOAN TO AGAIN	Y		N		

BORROWER AND INFO | ITEM LOANED

NOTES | CONDITION OF ITEM

DATE OUT

DATE BACK

		P	G	F	E
OUT					
BACK					
LOAN TO AGAIN	Y		N		

"We are of opinion that instead of letting books grow moldy behind an iron grating, far from the vulgar gaze, it is better to let them wear out by being read." Jules Verne

KEY FOR CONDITION OF ITEM P=POOR G=GOOD F=FAIR E=EXCELLENT

BORROWER AND INFO	ITEM LOANED

NOTES	CONDITION OF ITEM
DATE OUT DATE BACK	P G F E OUT ☐☐☐☐ BACK ☐☐☐☐ LOAN TO AGAIN Y ☐ N ☐

BORROWER AND INFO	ITEM LOANED

NOTES	CONDITION OF ITEM
DATE OUT DATE BACK	P G F E OUT ☐☐☐☐ BACK ☐☐☐☐ LOAN TO AGAIN Y ☐ N ☐

KEY FOR CONDITION OF ITEM P=POOR G=GOOD F=FAIR E=EXCELLENT

BORROWER AND INFO	ITEM LOANED

NOTES	CONDITION OF ITEM
DATE OUT DATE BACK	

	P	G	F	E
OUT				
BACK				
LOAN TO AGAIN	Y		N	

BORROWER AND INFO	ITEM LOANED

NOTES	CONDITION OF ITEM
DATE OUT DATE BACK	

	P	G	F	E
OUT				
BACK				
LOAN TO AGAIN	Y		N	

"Reading makes immigrants of us all. It takes us away from home, but more important, it finds homes for us everywhere."
Jean Rhys

KEY FOR CONDITION OF ITEM P=POOR G=GOOD F=FAIR E=EXCELLENT

BORROWER AND INFO	ITEM LOANED

NOTES	CONDITION OF ITEM
DATE OUT DATE BACK	P G F E OUT ☐ ☐ ☐ ☐ BACK ☐ ☐ ☐ ☐ LOAN TO AGAIN Y ☐ N ☐

BORROWER AND INFO	ITEM LOANED

NOTES	CONDITION OF ITEM
DATE OUT DATE BACK	P G F E OUT ☐ ☐ ☐ ☐ BACK ☐ ☐ ☐ ☐ LOAN TO AGAIN Y ☐ N ☐

KEY FOR CONDITION OF ITEM P=POOR G=GOOD F=FAIR E=EXCELLENT

BORROWER AND INFO | ITEM LOANED

NOTES

DATE OUT

DATE BACK

CONDITION OF ITEM

	P	G	F	E
OUT				
BACK				
LOAN TO AGAIN	Y		N	

BORROWER AND INFO | ITEM LOANED

NOTES

DATE OUT

DATE BACK

CONDITION OF ITEM

	P	G	F	E
OUT				
BACK				
LOAN TO AGAIN	Y		N	

"Books may well be the only true magic." Alice Hoffman

KEY FOR CONDITION OF ITEM P=POOR G=GOOD F=FAIR E=EXCELLENT

BORROWER AND INFO	ITEM LOANED

NOTES	CONDITION OF ITEM
DATE OUT DATE BACK	

	P	G	F	E
OUT				
BACK				

LOAN TO AGAIN Y N

BORROWER AND INFO	ITEM LOANED

NOTES	CONDITION OF ITEM
DATE OUT DATE BACK	

	P	G	F	E
OUT				
BACK				

LOAN TO AGAIN Y N

KEY FOR CONDITION OF ITEM P=POOR G=GOOD F=FAIR E=EXCELLENT

BORROWER AND INFO

ITEM LOANED

NOTES

DATE OUT

DATE BACK

CONDITION OF ITEM

	P	G	F	E
OUT				
BACK				

LOAN TO AGAIN	Y		N	

BORROWER AND INFO

ITEM LOANED

NOTES

DATE OUT

DATE BACK

CONDITION OF ITEM

	P	G	F	E
OUT				
BACK				

LOAN TO AGAIN	Y		N	

"In the end, we'll all become stories." Margaret Attwood

KEY FOR CONDITION OF ITEM P=POOR G=GOOD F=FAIR E=EXCELLENT

BORROWER AND INFO	ITEM LOANED

NOTES	CONDITION OF ITEM
DATE OUT DATE BACK	

	P	G	F	E
OUT				
BACK				
LOAN TO AGAIN	Y		N	

BORROWER AND INFO	ITEM LOANED

NOTES	CONDITION OF ITEM
DATE OUT DATE BACK	

	P	G	F	E
OUT				
BACK				
LOAN TO AGAIN	Y		N	

KEY FOR CONDITION OF ITEM P=POOR G=GOOD F=FAIR E=EXCELLENT

BORROWER AND INFO | ITEM LOANED

NOTES

DATE OUT

DATE BACK

CONDITION OF ITEM

	P	G	F	E
OUT				
BACK				
LOAN TO AGAIN	Y		N	

BORROWER AND INFO | ITEM LOANED

NOTES

DATE OUT

DATE BACK

CONDITION OF ITEM

	P	G	F	E
OUT				
BACK				
LOAN TO AGAIN	Y		N	

"Youth is a beautiful dream, on whose brightness books shed a blinding dust." *Khalil Gibran*

KEY FOR CONDITION OF ITEM P=POOR G=GOOD F=FAIR E=EXCELLENT

BORROWER AND INFO	ITEM LOANED

NOTES	CONDITION OF ITEM
DATE OUT DATE BACK	P G F E OUT ☐ ☐ ☐ ☐ BACK ☐ ☐ ☐ ☐ LOAN TO AGAIN Y ☐ N ☐

BORROWER AND INFO	ITEM LOANED

NOTES	CONDITION OF ITEM
DATE OUT DATE BACK	P G F E OUT ☐ ☐ ☐ ☐ BACK ☐ ☐ ☐ ☐ LOAN TO AGAIN Y ☐ N ☐

KEY FOR CONDITION OF ITEM P=POOR G=GOOD F=FAIR E=EXCELLENT

BORROWER AND INFO	ITEM LOANED

NOTES	CONDITION OF ITEM
DATE OUT DATE BACK	P G F E OUT ☐☐☐☐ BACK ☐☐☐☐ LOAN TO AGAIN Y ☐ N ☐

BORROWER AND INFO	ITEM LOANED

NOTES	CONDITION OF ITEM
DATE OUT DATE BACK	P G F E OUT ☐☐☐☐ BACK ☐☐☐☐ LOAN TO AGAIN Y ☐ N ☐

"If you would tell me the heart of a man, tell me not what he reads, but what he rereads." *François Mauriac*

KEY FOR CONDITION OF ITEM P=POOR G=GOOD F=FAIR E=EXCELLENT

BORROWER AND INFO	ITEM LOANED

NOTES	CONDITION OF ITEM
DATE OUT DATE BACK	P G F E OUT BACK LOAN TO AGAIN Y N

BORROWER AND INFO	ITEM LOANED

NOTES	CONDITION OF ITEM
DATE OUT DATE BACK	P G F E OUT BACK LOAN TO AGAIN Y N

KEY FOR CONDITION OF ITEM P=POOR G=GOOD F=FAIR E=EXCELLENT

BORROWER AND INFO | **ITEM LOANED**

BORROWER AND INFO	ITEM LOANED

NOTES	CONDITION OF ITEM				
DATE OUT		P	G	F	E
DATE BACK	OUT				
	BACK				
	LOAN TO AGAIN	Y		N	

BORROWER AND INFO	ITEM LOANED

NOTES	CONDITION OF ITEM				
DATE OUT		P	G	F	E
DATE BACK	OUT				
	BACK				
	LOAN TO AGAIN	Y		N	

"The reading of all good books is like a conversation with the finest minds of past centuries." Rene Descartes

KEY FOR CONDITION OF ITEM P=POOR G=GOOD F=FAIR E=EXCELLENT

BORROWER AND INFO	ITEM LOANED

NOTES	CONDITION OF ITEM
DATE OUT DATE BACK	

	P	G	F	E
OUT				
BACK				

LOAN TO AGAIN	Y		N	

BORROWER AND INFO	ITEM LOANED

NOTES	CONDITION OF ITEM
DATE OUT DATE BACK	

	P	G	F	E
OUT				
BACK				

LOAN TO AGAIN	Y		N	

KEY FOR CONDITION OF ITEM P=POOR G=GOOD F=FAIR E=EXCELLENT

BORROWER AND INFO | ITEM LOANED

NOTES

DATE OUT

DATE BACK

CONDITION OF ITEM

	P	G	F	E
OUT				
BACK				
LOAN TO AGAIN	Y		N	

BORROWER AND INFO | ITEM LOANED

NOTES

DATE OUT

DATE BACK

CONDITION OF ITEM

	P	G	F	E
OUT				
BACK				
LOAN TO AGAIN	Y		N	

"Classic' – a book which people praise and don't read."
Mark Twain

KEY FOR CONDITION OF ITEM P=POOR G=GOOD F=FAIR E=EXCELLENT

BORROWER AND INFO	ITEM LOANED

NOTES	CONDITION OF ITEM
DATE OUT DATE BACK	P G F E OUT ☐ ☐ ☐ ☐ BACK ☐ ☐ ☐ ☐ LOAN TO AGAIN Y ☐ N ☐

BORROWER AND INFO	ITEM LOANED

NOTES	CONDITION OF ITEM
DATE OUT DATE BACK	P G F E OUT ☐ ☐ ☐ ☐ BACK ☐ ☐ ☐ ☐ LOAN TO AGAIN Y ☐ N ☐

KEY FOR CONDITION OF ITEM P=POOR G=GOOD F=FAIR E=EXCELLENT

BORROWER AND INFO	ITEM LOANED

NOTES	CONDITION OF ITEM
DATE OUT DATE BACK	P G F E OUT ☐☐☐☐ BACK ☐☐☐☐ LOAN TO AGAIN Y ☐ N ☐

BORROWER AND INFO	ITEM LOANED

NOTES	CONDITION OF ITEM
DATE OUT DATE BACK	P G F E OUT ☐☐☐☐ BACK ☐☐☐☐ LOAN TO AGAIN Y ☐ N ☐

"What isn't said is as important as what is said."
Colson Whitehead

KEY FOR CONDITION OF ITEM P=POOR G=GOOD F=FAIR E=EXCELLENT

BORROWER AND INFO	ITEM LOANED

NOTES	CONDITION OF ITEM
DATE OUT DATE BACK	P G F E OUT BACK LOAN TO AGAIN Y N

BORROWER AND INFO	ITEM LOANED

NOTES	CONDITION OF ITEM
DATE OUT DATE BACK	P G F E OUT BACK LOAN TO AGAIN Y N

KEY FOR CONDITION OF ITEM P=POOR G=GOOD F=FAIR E=EXCELLENT

BORROWER AND INFO	ITEM LOANED

NOTES	CONDITION OF ITEM
DATE OUT DATE BACK	P G F E OUT BACK LOAN TO AGAIN Y N

BORROWER AND INFO	ITEM LOANED

NOTES	CONDITION OF ITEM
DATE OUT DATE BACK	P G F E OUT BACK LOAN TO AGAIN Y N

"Happiness is the smell of a new book."
unknown & many

KEY FOR CONDITION OF ITEM P=POOR G=GOOD F=FAIR E=EXCELLENT

BORROWER AND INFO	ITEM LOANED

NOTES	CONDITION OF ITEM
DATE OUT DATE BACK	

	P	G	F	E
OUT				
BACK				
LOAN TO AGAIN	Y		N	

BORROWER AND INFO	ITEM LOANED

NOTES	CONDITION OF ITEM
DATE OUT DATE BACK	

	P	G	F	E
OUT				
BACK				
LOAN TO AGAIN	Y		N	

KEY FOR CONDITION OF ITEM P=POOR G=GOOD F=FAIR E=EXCELLENT

BORROWER AND INFO	ITEM LOANED

NOTES	CONDITION OF ITEM
DATE OUT DATE BACK	P G F E OUT ☐☐☐☐ BACK ☐☐☐☐ LOAN TO AGAIN Y ☐ N ☐

BORROWER AND INFO	ITEM LOANED

NOTES	CONDITION OF ITEM
DATE OUT DATE BACK	P G F E OUT ☐☐☐☐ BACK ☐☐☐☐ LOAN TO AGAIN Y ☐ N ☐

"So please, oh please, we beg, we pray, go throw your TV set away, and in its place you can install a lovely bookshelf on the wall." Ronald Dahl

KEY FOR CONDITION OF ITEM P=POOR G=GOOD F=FAIR E=EXCELLENT

BORROWER AND INFO	ITEM LOANED

NOTES	CONDITION OF ITEM
DATE OUT DATE BACK	

	P	G	F	E
OUT				
BACK				
LOAN TO AGAIN	Y		N	

BORROWER AND INFO	ITEM LOANED

NOTES	CONDITION OF ITEM
DATE OUT DATE BACK	

	P	G	F	E
OUT				
BACK				
LOAN TO AGAIN	Y		N	

KEY FOR CONDITION OF ITEM P=POOR G=GOOD F=FAIR E=EXCELLENT

BORROWER AND INFO	ITEM LOANED

NOTES	CONDITION OF ITEM
DATE OUT DATE BACK	P G F E OUT BACK LOAN TO AGAIN Y N

BORROWER AND INFO	ITEM LOANED

NOTES	CONDITION OF ITEM
DATE OUT DATE BACK	P G F E OUT BACK LOAN TO AGAIN Y N

"Books serve to show a man that those original thoughts of his aren't very new after all." Abraham Lincoln

KEY FOR CONDITION OF ITEM P=POOR G=GOOD F=FAIR E=EXCELLENT

BORROWER AND INFO	ITEM LOANED

NOTES	CONDITION OF ITEM
DATE OUT DATE BACK	P G F E OUT ☐☐☐☐ BACK ☐☐☐☐ LOAN TO AGAIN Y ☐ N ☐

BORROWER AND INFO	ITEM LOANED

NOTES	CONDITION OF ITEM
DATE OUT DATE BACK	P G F E OUT ☐☐☐☐ BACK ☐☐☐☐ LOAN TO AGAIN Y ☐ N ☐

KEY FOR CONDITION OF ITEM P=POOR G=GOOD F=FAIR E=EXCELLENT

BORROWER AND INFO

ITEM LOANED

NOTES

DATE OUT

DATE BACK

CONDITION OF ITEM

	P	G	F	E
OUT				
BACK				

LOAN TO AGAIN Y N

BORROWER AND INFO

ITEM LOANED

NOTES

DATE OUT

DATE BACK

CONDITION OF ITEM

	P	G	F	E
OUT				
BACK				

LOAN TO AGAIN Y N

"If you don't see the book you want on the shelf, write it."
Beverly Cleary

KEY FOR CONDITION OF ITEM P=POOR G=GOOD F=FAIR E=EXCELLENT

BORROWER AND INFO	ITEM LOANED

NOTES	CONDITION OF ITEM
DATE OUT DATE BACK	

	P	G	F	E
OUT				
BACK				
LOAN TO AGAIN	Y		N	

BORROWER AND INFO	ITEM LOANED

NOTES	CONDITION OF ITEM
DATE OUT DATE BACK	

	P	G	F	E
OUT				
BACK				
LOAN TO AGAIN	Y		N	

KEY FOR CONDITION OF ITEM P=POOR G=GOOD F=FAIR E=EXCELLENT

BORROWER AND INFO	ITEM LOANED

NOTES	CONDITION OF ITEM				
DATE OUT DATE BACK		P	G	F	E
	OUT				
	BACK				
	LOAN TO AGAIN	Y		N	

BORROWER AND INFO	ITEM LOANED

NOTES	CONDITION OF ITEM				
DATE OUT DATE BACK		P	G	F	E
	OUT				
	BACK				
	LOAN TO AGAIN	Y		N	

"Once you learn to read, you will be forever free."
Frederick Douglass

KEY FOR CONDITION OF ITEM P=POOR G=GOOD F=FAIR E=EXCELLENT

BORROWER AND INFO	ITEM LOANED

NOTES	CONDITION OF ITEM
DATE OUT DATE BACK	P G F E OUT ☐☐☐☐ BACK ☐☐☐☐ LOAN TO AGAIN Y ☐ N ☐

BORROWER AND INFO	ITEM LOANED

NOTES	CONDITION OF ITEM
DATE OUT DATE BACK	P G F E OUT ☐☐☐☐ BACK ☐☐☐☐ LOAN TO AGAIN Y ☐ N ☐

KEY FOR CONDITION OF ITEM P=POOR G=GOOD F=FAIR E=EXCELLENT

BORROWER AND INFO	ITEM LOANED

NOTES	CONDITION OF ITEM
DATE OUT DATE BACK	P G F E OUT ☐☐☐☐ BACK ☐☐☐☐ LOAN TO AGAIN Y ☐ N ☐

BORROWER AND INFO	ITEM LOANED

NOTES	CONDITION OF ITEM
DATE OUT DATE BACK	P G F E OUT ☐☐☐☐ BACK ☐☐☐☐ LOAN TO AGAIN Y ☐ N ☐

"We read to know we are not alone." *C.S. Lewis*

KEY FOR CONDITION OF ITEM P=POOR G=GOOD F=FAIR E=EXCELLENT

BORROWER AND INFO	ITEM LOANED

NOTES	CONDITION OF ITEM
DATE OUT DATE BACK	P G F E OUT ☐ ☐ ☐ ☐ BACK ☐ ☐ ☐ ☐ LOAN TO AGAIN Y ☐ N ☐

BORROWER AND INFO	ITEM LOANED

NOTES	CONDITION OF ITEM
DATE OUT DATE BACK	P G F E OUT ☐ ☐ ☐ ☐ BACK ☐ ☐ ☐ ☐ LOAN TO AGAIN Y ☐ N ☐

KEY FOR CONDITION OF ITEM P=POOR G=GOOD F=FAIR E=EXCELLENT

BORROWER AND INFO

ITEM LOANED

NOTES

DATE OUT

DATE BACK

CONDITION OF ITEM

	P	G	F	E
OUT				
BACK				

LOAN TO AGAIN Y N

BORROWER AND INFO

ITEM LOANED

NOTES

DATE OUT

DATE BACK

CONDITION OF ITEM

	P	G	F	E
OUT				
BACK				

LOAN TO AGAIN Y N

"I find television very educating. Every time somebody turns on the set, I go into the other room and read a book" Groucho Marx

KEY FOR CONDITION OF ITEM P=POOR G=GOOD F=FAIR E=EXCELLENT

BORROWER AND INFO	ITEM LOANED

NOTES	CONDITION OF ITEM
DATE OUT DATE BACK	P G F E OUT BACK LOAN TO AGAIN Y N

BORROWER AND INFO	ITEM LOANED

NOTES	CONDITION OF ITEM
DATE OUT DATE BACK	P G F E OUT BACK LOAN TO AGAIN Y N

KEY FOR CONDITION OF ITEM P=POOR G=GOOD F=FAIR E=EXCELLENT

BORROWER AND INFO | ITEM LOANED

NOTES

DATE OUT

DATE BACK

CONDITION OF ITEM

	P	G	F	E
OUT				
BACK				

LOAN TO AGAIN Y N

BORROWER AND INFO | ITEM LOANED

NOTES

DATE OUT

DATE BACK

CONDITION OF ITEM

	P	G	F	E
OUT				
BACK				

LOAN TO AGAIN Y N

"Some books leave us free and some books make us free." Ralph Waldo Emerson

KEY FOR CONDITION OF ITEM P=POOR G=GOOD F=FAIR E=EXCELLENT

BORROWER AND INFO	ITEM LOANED

NOTES	CONDITION OF ITEM
DATE OUT DATE BACK	P G F E OUT ☐☐☐☐ BACK ☐☐☐☐ LOAN TO AGAIN Y ☐ N ☐

BORROWER AND INFO	ITEM LOANED

NOTES	CONDITION OF ITEM
DATE OUT DATE BACK	P G F E OUT ☐☐☐☐ BACK ☐☐☐☐ LOAN TO AGAIN Y ☐ N ☐

KEY FOR CONDITION OF ITEM P=POOR G=GOOD F=FAIR E=EXCELLENT

BORROWER AND INFO | ITEM LOANED

NOTES

DATE OUT

DATE BACK

CONDITION OF ITEM

	P	G	F	E
OUT				
BACK				
LOAN TO AGAIN	Y		N	

BORROWER AND INFO | ITEM LOANED

NOTES

DATE OUT

DATE BACK

CONDITION OF ITEM

	P	G	F	E
OUT				
BACK				
LOAN TO AGAIN	Y		N	

"You know you've read a good book when you turn the last page and feel a little as if you have lost a friend." Paul Sweeney

KEY FOR CONDITION OF ITEM P=POOR G=GOOD F=FAIR E=EXCELLENT

BORROWER AND INFO	ITEM LOANED

NOTES	CONDITION OF ITEM
DATE OUT DATE BACK	P G F E OUT ☐ ☐ ☐ ☐ BACK ☐ ☐ ☐ ☐ LOAN TO AGAIN Y ☐ N ☐

BORROWER AND INFO	ITEM LOANED

NOTES	CONDITION OF ITEM
DATE OUT DATE BACK	P G F E OUT ☐ ☐ ☐ ☐ BACK ☐ ☐ ☐ ☐ LOAN TO AGAIN Y ☐ N ☐

KEY FOR CONDITION OF ITEM P=POOR G=GOOD F=FAIR E=EXCELLENT

BORROWER AND INFO	ITEM LOANED

NOTES	CONDITION OF ITEM
DATE OUT DATE BACK	P G F E OUT ☐☐☐☐ BACK ☐☐☐☐ LOAN TO AGAIN Y ☐ N ☐

BORROWER AND INFO	ITEM LOANED

NOTES	CONDITION OF ITEM
DATE OUT DATE BACK	P G F E OUT ☐☐☐☐ BACK ☐☐☐☐ LOAN TO AGAIN Y ☐ N ☐

"The more that you read, the more things you will know. The more that you learn, the more places you'll go." Dr. Seuss

KEY FOR CONDITION OF ITEM P=POOR G=GOOD F=FAIR E=EXCELLENT

BORROWER AND INFO	ITEM LOANED

NOTES	CONDITION OF ITEM
DATE OUT DATE BACK	P G F E OUT BACK LOAN TO AGAIN Y N

BORROWER AND INFO	ITEM LOANED

NOTES	CONDITION OF ITEM
DATE OUT DATE BACK	P G F E OUT BACK LOAN TO AGAIN Y N

KEY FOR CONDITION OF ITEM P=POOR G=GOOD F=FAIR E=EXCELLENT

BORROWER AND INFO	ITEM LOANED

NOTES	CONDITION OF ITEM
DATE OUT DATE BACK	P G F E OUT BACK LOAN TO AGAIN Y N

BORROWER AND INFO	ITEM LOANED

NOTES	CONDITION OF ITEM
DATE OUT DATE BACK	P G F E OUT BACK LOAN TO AGAIN Y N

"The best books... are those that tell you what you know already." *George Orwell*

KEY FOR CONDITION OF ITEM P=POOR G=GOOD F=FAIR E=EXCELLENT

BORROWER AND INFO	ITEM LOANED

NOTES	CONDITION OF ITEM
DATE OUT DATE BACK	P G F E OUT BACK LOAN TO AGAIN Y N

BORROWER AND INFO	ITEM LOANED

NOTES	CONDITION OF ITEM
DATE OUT DATE BACK	P G F E OUT BACK LOAN TO AGAIN Y N

KEY FOR CONDITION OF ITEM P=POOR G=GOOD F=FAIR E=EXCELLENT

BORROWER AND INFO	ITEM LOANED

NOTES	CONDITION OF ITEM
DATE OUT DATE BACK	P G F E OUT BACK LOAN TO AGAIN Y N

BORROWER AND INFO	ITEM LOANED

NOTES	CONDITION OF ITEM
DATE OUT DATE BACK	P G F E OUT BACK LOAN TO AGAIN Y N

"Reading has been the chief pleasure of my life. Indeed, reading has meant so much to me that I am in danger of extravagance whenever I speak of it." Helen Keller

KEY FOR CONDITION OF ITEM P=POOR G=GOOD F=FAIR E=EXCELLENT

BORROWER AND INFO | ITEM LOANED

NOTES

DATE OUT

DATE BACK

CONDITION OF ITEM

	P	G	F	E
OUT				
BACK				
LOAN TO AGAIN	Y		N	

BORROWER AND INFO | ITEM LOANED

NOTES

DATE OUT

DATE BACK

CONDITION OF ITEM

	P	G	F	E
OUT				
BACK				
LOAN TO AGAIN	Y		N	

KEY FOR CONDITION OF ITEM P=POOR G=GOOD F=FAIR E=EXCELLENT

BORROWER AND INFO	ITEM LOANED

NOTES	CONDITION OF ITEM
DATE OUT DATE BACK	P G F E OUT BACK LOAN TO AGAIN Y N

BORROWER AND INFO	ITEM LOANED

NOTES	CONDITION OF ITEM
DATE OUT DATE BACK	P G F E OUT BACK LOAN TO AGAIN Y N

"Many a book is like a key to unknown chambers within the castle of one's own self." Franz Kafka

KEY FOR CONDITION OF ITEM P=POOR G=GOOD F=FAIR E=EXCELLENT

BORROWER AND INFO	ITEM LOANED

NOTES	CONDITION OF ITEM				
DATE OUT		P	G	F	E
DATE BACK	OUT				
	BACK				
	LOAN TO AGAIN	Y		N	

BORROWER AND INFO	ITEM LOANED

NOTES	CONDITION OF ITEM				
DATE OUT		P	G	F	E
DATE BACK	OUT				
	BACK				
	LOAN TO AGAIN	Y		N	

KEY FOR CONDITION OF ITEM P=POOR G=GOOD F=FAIR E=EXCELLENT

BORROWER AND INFO	ITEM LOANED

NOTES	CONDITION OF ITEM
DATE OUT DATE BACK	P G F E OUT BACK LOAN TO AGAIN Y N

BORROWER AND INFO	ITEM LOANED

NOTES	CONDITION OF ITEM
DATE OUT DATE BACK	P G F E OUT BACK LOAN TO AGAIN Y N

"Reading is a conversation. All books talk. But a good book listens as well." Mark Haddon

KEY FOR CONDITION OF ITEM P=POOR G=GOOD F=FAIR E=EXCELLENT

BORROWER AND INFO

ITEM LOANED

NOTES

DATE OUT

DATE BACK

CONDITION OF ITEM

	P	G	F	E
OUT				
BACK				

LOAN TO AGAIN Y N

BORROWER AND INFO

ITEM LOANED

NOTES

DATE OUT

DATE BACK

CONDITION OF ITEM

	P	G	F	E
OUT				
BACK				

LOAN TO AGAIN Y N

KEY FOR CONDITION OF ITEM P=POOR G=GOOD F=FAIR E=EXCELLENT

BORROWER AND INFO	ITEM LOANED

NOTES	CONDITION OF ITEM
DATE OUT DATE BACK	

	P	G	F	E
OUT				
BACK				

LOAN TO AGAIN	Y		N	

BORROWER AND INFO	ITEM LOANED

NOTES	CONDITION OF ITEM
DATE OUT DATE BACK	

	P	G	F	E
OUT				
BACK				

LOAN TO AGAIN	Y		N	

"There is more treasure in books than in all the pirate's loot on Treasure Island." Walt Disney

KEY FOR CONDITION OF ITEM P=POOR G=GOOD F=FAIR E=EXCELLENT

BORROWER AND INFO | ITEM LOANED

NOTES

DATE OUT

DATE BACK

CONDITION OF ITEM

	P	G	F	E
OUT				
BACK				

LOAN TO AGAIN Y N

BORROWER AND INFO | ITEM LOANED

NOTES

DATE OUT

DATE BACK

CONDITION OF ITEM

	P	G	F	E
OUT				
BACK				

LOAN TO AGAIN Y N

KEY FOR CONDITION OF ITEM P=POOR G=GOOD F=FAIR E=EXCELLENT

BORROWER AND INFO	ITEM LOANED

NOTES	CONDITION OF ITEM
DATE OUT DATE BACK	

	P	G	F	E
OUT				
BACK				
LOAN TO AGAIN	Y		N	

BORROWER AND INFO	ITEM LOANED

NOTES	CONDITION OF ITEM
DATE OUT DATE BACK	

	P	G	F	E
OUT				
BACK				
LOAN TO AGAIN	Y		N	

"Reading is essential for those who seek to rise above the ordinary." Jim Rohn

KEY FOR CONDITION OF ITEM P=POOR G=GOOD F=FAIR E=EXCELLENT

BORROWER AND INFO	ITEM LOANED

NOTES	CONDITION OF ITEM
DATE OUT DATE BACK	P G F E OUT ☐ ☐ ☐ ☐ BACK ☐ ☐ ☐ ☐ LOAN TO AGAIN Y ☐ N ☐

BORROWER AND INFO	ITEM LOANED

NOTES	CONDITION OF ITEM
DATE OUT DATE BACK	P G F E OUT ☐ ☐ ☐ ☐ BACK ☐ ☐ ☐ ☐ LOAN TO AGAIN Y ☐ N ☐

KEY FOR CONDITION OF ITEM P=POOR G=GOOD F=FAIR E=EXCELLENT

BORROWER AND INFO	ITEM LOANED

NOTES	CONDITION OF ITEM
DATE OUT DATE BACK	P G F E OUT ☐ ☐ ☐ ☐ BACK ☐ ☐ ☐ ☐ LOAN TO AGAIN Y ☐ N ☐

BORROWER AND INFO	ITEM LOANED

NOTES	CONDITION OF ITEM
DATE OUT DATE BACK	P G F E OUT ☐ ☐ ☐ ☐ BACK ☐ ☐ ☐ ☐ LOAN TO AGAIN Y ☐ N ☐

"I can feel infinitely alive curled up on the sofa reading a book." Benedict Cumberbatch

KEY FOR CONDITION OF ITEM P=POOR G=GOOD F=FAIR E=EXCELLENT

BORROWER AND INFO

ITEM LOANED

NOTES

DATE OUT

DATE BACK

CONDITION OF ITEM

	P	G	F	E
OUT				
BACK				
LOAN TO AGAIN	Y		N	

BORROWER AND INFO

ITEM LOANED

NOTES

DATE OUT

DATE BACK

CONDITION OF ITEM

	P	G	F	E
OUT				
BACK				
LOAN TO AGAIN	Y		N	

KEY FOR CONDITION OF ITEM P=POOR G=GOOD F=FAIR E=EXCELLENT

BORROWER AND INFO	ITEM LOANED

NOTES	CONDITION OF ITEM
DATE OUT DATE BACK	P G F E OUT ☐☐☐☐ BACK ☐☐☐☐ LOAN TO AGAIN Y ☐ N ☐

BORROWER AND INFO	ITEM LOANED

NOTES	CONDITION OF ITEM
DATE OUT DATE BACK	P G F E OUT ☐☐☐☐ BACK ☐☐☐☐ LOAN TO AGAIN Y ☐ N ☐

"Let us remember: One book, one pen, one child, and one teacher can change the world." Malala Yousafzai

KEY FOR CONDITION OF ITEM P=POOR G=GOOD F=FAIR E=EXCELLENT

BORROWER AND INFO	ITEM LOANED

NOTES	CONDITION OF ITEM
DATE OUT DATE BACK	P G F E OUT ☐ ☐ ☐ ☐ BACK ☐ ☐ ☐ ☐ LOAN TO AGAIN Y ☐ N ☐

BORROWER AND INFO	ITEM LOANED

NOTES	CONDITION OF ITEM
DATE OUT DATE BACK	P G F E OUT ☐ ☐ ☐ ☐ BACK ☐ ☐ ☐ ☐ LOAN TO AGAIN Y ☐ N ☐

KEY FOR CONDITION OF ITEM P=POOR G=GOOD F=FAIR E=EXCELLENT

BORROWER AND INFO	ITEM LOANED

NOTES	CONDITION OF ITEM
DATE OUT DATE BACK	P G F E OUT BACK LOAN TO AGAIN Y N

BORROWER AND INFO	ITEM LOANED

NOTES	CONDITION OF ITEM
DATE OUT DATE BACK	P G F E OUT BACK LOAN TO AGAIN Y N

"Once you've read a book you care about, some part of it is always with you." Louis L'Amour

KEY FOR CONDITION OF ITEM P=POOR G=GOOD F=FAIR E=EXCELLENT

BORROWER AND INFO	ITEM LOANED

NOTES	CONDITION OF ITEM
DATE OUT DATE BACK	

	P	G	F	E
OUT				
BACK				
LOAN TO AGAIN	Y		N	

BORROWER AND INFO	ITEM LOANED

NOTES	CONDITION OF ITEM
DATE OUT DATE BACK	

	P	G	F	E
OUT				
BACK				
LOAN TO AGAIN	Y		N	

KEY FOR CONDITION OF ITEM P=POOR G=GOOD F=FAIR E=EXCELLENT

BORROWER AND INFO	ITEM LOANED

NOTES	CONDITION OF ITEM
DATE OUT DATE BACK	P G F E OUT ☐☐☐☐ BACK ☐☐☐☐ LOAN TO AGAIN Y ☐ N ☐

BORROWER AND INFO	ITEM LOANED

NOTES	CONDITION OF ITEM
DATE OUT DATE BACK	P G F E OUT ☐☐☐☐ BACK ☐☐☐☐ LOAN TO AGAIN Y ☐ N ☐

"Books are my friends." Saoirse (age 6)

KEY FOR CONDITION OF ITEM P=POOR G=GOOD F=FAIR E=EXCELLENT

BORROWER AND INFO	ITEM LOANED

NOTES	CONDITION OF ITEM
DATE OUT DATE BACK	P G F E OUT ☐ ☐ ☐ ☐ BACK ☐ ☐ ☐ ☐ LOAN TO AGAIN Y ☐ N ☐

BORROWER AND INFO	ITEM LOANED

NOTES	CONDITION OF ITEM
DATE OUT DATE BACK	P G F E OUT ☐ ☐ ☐ ☐ BACK ☐ ☐ ☐ ☐ LOAN TO AGAIN Y ☐ N ☐

KEY FOR CONDITION OF ITEM P=POOR G=GOOD F=FAIR E=EXCELLENT

BORROWER AND INFO | ITEM LOANED

BORROWER AND INFO	ITEM LOANED

NOTES	CONDITION OF ITEM
DATE OUT DATE BACK	P G F E OUT ☐☐☐☐ BACK ☐☐☐☐ LOAN TO AGAIN Y ☐ N ☐

BORROWER AND INFO	ITEM LOANED

NOTES	CONDITION OF ITEM
DATE OUT DATE BACK	P G F E OUT ☐☐☐☐ BACK ☐☐☐☐ LOAN TO AGAIN Y ☐ N ☐

"Maybe this is why we read, and why in moments of darkness we return to books: to find words for what we already know." Alberto Manguel

KEY FOR CONDITION OF ITEM P=POOR G=GOOD F=FAIR E=EXCELLENT

BORROWER AND INFO	ITEM LOANED

NOTES	CONDITION OF ITEM
DATE OUT DATE BACK	P G F E OUT ☐☐☐☐ BACK ☐☐☐☐ LOAN TO AGAIN Y ☐ N ☐

BORROWER AND INFO	ITEM LOANED

NOTES	CONDITION OF ITEM
DATE OUT DATE BACK	P G F E OUT ☐☐☐☐ BACK ☐☐☐☐ LOAN TO AGAIN Y ☐ N ☐

KEY FOR CONDITION OF ITEM P=POOR G=GOOD F=FAIR E=EXCELLENT

BORROWER AND INFO	ITEM LOANED

NOTES	CONDITION OF ITEM
DATE OUT DATE BACK	P G F E OUT ☐ ☐ ☐ ☐ BACK ☐ ☐ ☐ ☐ LOAN TO AGAIN Y ☐ N ☐

BORROWER AND INFO	ITEM LOANED

NOTES	CONDITION OF ITEM
DATE OUT DATE BACK	P G F E OUT ☐ ☐ ☐ ☐ BACK ☐ ☐ ☐ ☐ LOAN TO AGAIN Y ☐ N ☐

"The magic is only in what books say, how they stitched the patches of the universe together into one garment for us."

Ray Bradbury

KEY FOR CONDITION OF ITEM P=POOR G=GOOD F=FAIR E=EXCELLENT

BORROWER AND INFO	ITEM LOANED

NOTES	CONDITION OF ITEM
DATE OUT DATE BACK	P G F E OUT ☐ ☐ ☐ ☐ BACK ☐ ☐ ☐ ☐ LOAN TO AGAIN Y ☐ N ☐

BORROWER AND INFO	ITEM LOANED

NOTES	CONDITION OF ITEM
DATE OUT DATE BACK	P G F E OUT ☐ ☐ ☐ ☐ BACK ☐ ☐ ☐ ☐ LOAN TO AGAIN Y ☐ N ☐

KEY FOR CONDITION OF ITEM P=POOR G=GOOD F=FAIR E=EXCELLENT

BORROWER AND INFO	ITEM LOANED

NOTES	CONDITION OF ITEM
DATE OUT DATE BACK	P G F E OUT ☐ ☐ ☐ ☐ BACK ☐ ☐ ☐ ☐ LOAN TO AGAIN Y ☐ N ☐

BORROWER AND INFO	ITEM LOANED

NOTES	CONDITION OF ITEM
DATE OUT DATE BACK	P G F E OUT ☐ ☐ ☐ ☐ BACK ☐ ☐ ☐ ☐ LOAN TO AGAIN Y ☐ N ☐

"Make it a rule never to give a child a book you would not read yourself." George Bernard Shaw

KEY FOR CONDITION OF ITEM P=POOR G=GOOD F=FAIR E=EXCELLENT

BORROWER AND INFO	ITEM LOANED

NOTES	CONDITION OF ITEM
DATE OUT DATE BACK	

	P	G	F	E
OUT				
BACK				

LOAN TO AGAIN	Y		N	

BORROWER AND INFO	ITEM LOANED

NOTES	CONDITION OF ITEM
DATE OUT DATE BACK	

	P	G	F	E
OUT				
BACK				

LOAN TO AGAIN	Y		N	

KEY FOR CONDITION OF ITEM P=POOR G=GOOD F=FAIR E=EXCELLENT

BORROWER AND INFO	ITEM LOANED

NOTES	CONDITION OF ITEM
DATE OUT DATE BACK	P G F E OUT ☐ ☐ ☐ ☐ BACK ☐ ☐ ☐ ☐ LOAN TO AGAIN Y ☐ N ☐

BORROWER AND INFO	ITEM LOANED

NOTES	CONDITION OF ITEM
DATE OUT DATE BACK	P G F E OUT ☐ ☐ ☐ ☐ BACK ☐ ☐ ☐ ☐ LOAN TO AGAIN Y ☐ N ☐

"Think before you speak. Read before you think."
Fran Lebowitz

KEY FOR CONDITION OF ITEM P=POOR G=GOOD F=FAIR E=EXCELLENT

BORROWER AND INFO | ITEM LOANED

NOTES

DATE OUT

DATE BACK

CONDITION OF ITEM

	P	G	F	E
OUT				
BACK				

LOAN TO AGAIN Y N

BORROWER AND INFO | ITEM LOANED

NOTES

DATE OUT

DATE BACK

CONDITION OF ITEM

	P	G	F	E
OUT				
BACK				

LOAN TO AGAIN Y N

KEY FOR CONDITION OF ITEM P=POOR G=GOOD F=FAIR E=EXCELLENT

BORROWER AND INFO	ITEM LOANED

NOTES	CONDITION OF ITEM
DATE OUT DATE BACK	P G F E OUT BACK LOAN TO AGAIN Y N

BORROWER AND INFO	ITEM LOANED

NOTES	CONDITION OF ITEM
DATE OUT DATE BACK	P G F E OUT BACK LOAN TO AGAIN Y N

"The person who deserves most pity is a lonesome one on a rainy day who doesn't know how to read." Benjamin Franklin

KEY FOR CONDITION OF ITEM P=POOR G=GOOD F=FAIR E=EXCELLENT

BORROWER AND INFO	ITEM LOANED

NOTES	CONDITION OF ITEM
DATE OUT DATE BACK	P G F E OUT BACK LOAN TO AGAIN Y N

BORROWER AND INFO	ITEM LOANED

NOTES	CONDITION OF ITEM
DATE OUT DATE BACK	P G F E OUT BACK LOAN TO AGAIN Y N

KEY FOR CONDITION OF ITEM P=POOR G=GOOD F=FAIR E=EXCELLENT

BORROWER AND INFO	ITEM LOANED

NOTES	CONDITION OF ITEM
DATE OUT DATE BACK	P G F E OUT BACK LOAN TO AGAIN Y N

BORROWER AND INFO	ITEM LOANED

NOTES	CONDITION OF ITEM
DATE OUT DATE BACK	P G F E OUT BACK LOAN TO AGAIN Y N

"That's the thing about books. They let you travel without moving your feet." Jhumpa Lahiri

KEY FOR CONDITION OF ITEM P=POOR G=GOOD F=FAIR E=EXCELLENT

BORROWER AND INFO	ITEM LOANED

NOTES	CONDITION OF ITEM
DATE OUT DATE BACK	P G F E OUT ☐☐☐☐ BACK ☐☐☐☐ LOAN TO AGAIN Y ☐ N ☐

BORROWER AND INFO	ITEM LOANED

NOTES	CONDITION OF ITEM
DATE OUT DATE BACK	P G F E OUT ☐☐☐☐ BACK ☐☐☐☐ LOAN TO AGAIN Y ☐ N ☐

KEY FOR CONDITION OF ITEM P=POOR G=GOOD F=FAIR E=EXCELLENT

BORROWER AND INFO	ITEM LOANED

NOTES	CONDITION OF ITEM
DATE OUT DATE BACK	P G F E OUT BACK LOAN TO AGAIN Y N

BORROWER AND INFO	ITEM LOANED

NOTES	CONDITION OF ITEM
DATE OUT DATE BACK	P G F E OUT BACK LOAN TO AGAIN Y N

"The world was hers for the reading." Betty Smith

KEY FOR CONDITION OF ITEM P=POOR G=GOOD F=FAIR E=EXCELLENT

BORROWER AND INFO	ITEM LOANED

NOTES	CONDITION OF ITEM
DATE OUT DATE BACK	P G F E OUT ☐☐☐☐ BACK ☐☐☐☐ LOAN TO AGAIN Y ☐ N ☐

BORROWER AND INFO	ITEM LOANED

NOTES	CONDITION OF ITEM
DATE OUT DATE BACK	P G F E OUT ☐☐☐☐ BACK ☐☐☐☐ LOAN TO AGAIN Y ☐ N ☐

KEY FOR CONDITION OF ITEM P=POOR G=GOOD F=FAIR E=EXCELLENT

BORROWER AND INFO | ITEM LOANED

NOTES

DATE OUT

DATE BACK

CONDITION OF ITEM

	P	G	F	E
OUT				
BACK				
LOAN TO AGAIN	Y		N	

BORROWER AND INFO | ITEM LOANED

NOTES

DATE OUT

DATE BACK

CONDITION OF ITEM

	P	G	F	E
OUT				
BACK				
LOAN TO AGAIN	Y		N	

"I kept always two books in my pocket, one to read, one to write in." Robert Louis Stevenson

KEY FOR CONDITION OF ITEM P=POOR G=GOOD F=FAIR E=EXCELLENT

RESORCES

https://celadonbooks.com/inspiring-quotes-about-books-and-reading/

The Grand Theater Blackpool

https://www.blackpoolgrand.co.uk/famous-quotes-about-reading#:~:text=%E2%80%9CBooks%20serve%20to%20show%20a,t%20very%20new%20after%20all.%E2%80%9D&text=%E2%80%9CThe%20man%20who%20does%20not,man%20who%20can't.%E2%80%9D&text=%E2%80%9CShow%20me%20a%20family%20of,people%20who%20move%20the%20world.%E2%80%9D&text=%E2%80%9CI%20guess%20there%20are%20never%20enough%20books.%E2%80%9D

https://www.goodhousekeeping.com/life/entertainment/g1640/book-lovers-quotes/?utm_source=google&utm_medium=cpc&utm_campaign=mgu_ga_ghk_md_pmx_hybd_mix_us_19597983321&gad_source=1&gclid=CjwKCAiAhP67BhAVEiwA2E_9g9fnR9Bk0gxstSA7mns_LbppCOUS81OA15RdbFokEM5EDfucp8C_mxoCX3oQAvD_BwE

https://www.afb.org/about-afb/history/helen-keller/helen-keller-quotes/helen-keller-quotes-reading

Made in the USA
Monee, IL
12 November 2026

c8efcecd-7b4d-45e3-a22d-016180a324b2R01